MORE SIGN & SAY

Bible Verses for Children

ILLUSTRATED BY Robert S. Jones
EDITED BY Daphna Flegal

 Abingdon Press

Nashville

More Sign and Say Bible Verses for Children

Copyright © 2000 Abingdon Press

All rights reserved.

ISBN 0-687-01457-3

00 01 02 03 04 05 06 07 08 09 – 10 9 8 7 6 5 4 3 2 1

MANUFACTURED IN THE UNITED STATES OF AMERICA

Sign, Say, and Remember

Children remember more easily what they learn when you involve both their bodies and their minds—and we want them to remember Bible verses! *More Sign and Say Bible Verses for Children* will help your children learn Bible verses using the hand motions of American Sign Language. Use the simple steps listed below to learn these verses yourself and then teach the verses to your children.

- Look at the illustrations.
- Read the written directions.
- Practice, practice, practice! (You need to be able to sign the verse for the children without looking at the page.)

© 1998 Abingdon Press

Thank you to Bob Geldreich and Peggy Jennings for their help with signing.

3

Contents

Old Testament

New Testament

Indexes

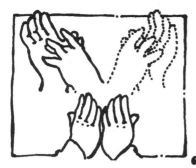

Then God commanded, "Let there be light."

BIBLE VERSE:

Genesis 1:3, *Good News Bible*

God — Point the index finger of your right hand, with the other fingers curled down. Bring the hand down and open the palm.

Commanded — Point the first finger of your right hand to your mouth. Turn the finger out and then down. Make the motion strong.

Light — Bring both hands in front of your body, with the finger-tips touching the thumbs. Move the hands up and apart in front of each shoulder. Open your hands and spread the fingers apart as you move.

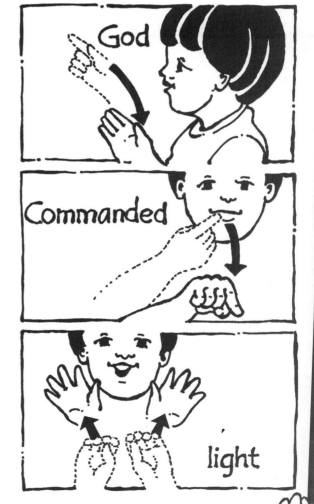

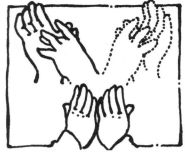

BIBLE VERSE:

And God saw that it was good.

Genesis 1:25

God — Point the index finger of your right hand, with the other fingers curled down. Bring the hand down and open the palm.

Saw — Hold your fingers in a V-shape in front of your eyes. Move the hand forward.

Good — Touch the fingers of your right hand to the lips. Move the hand forward and drop it into the open palm of the left hand.

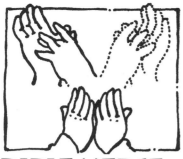

BIBLE VERSE:

9/24/00

Respect your father and your mother.

Exodus 20:12,
Good News Bible

Respect — Cross your first two fingers and touch your thumb to your last two fingers. This will make the letter "R." Bring the "R" in front of your face and down.

Respect

Father — Hold your right hand with the fingers spread apart. Touch the tip of the thumb to your forehead two times.

Father

Mother — Hold your right hand with the fingers spread apart. Touch the tip of the thumb to your chin two times.

Mother

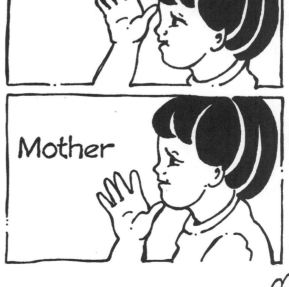

10/15/00 –
10/22/00

BIBLE VERSE:

God is with you
wherever you go.

Joshua 1:9

God — Point the index finger of your right hand, with the other fingers curled down. Bring the hand down and open the palm.

With — Hold both hands in fists, with the thumbs on the outside. Place the fists together, with the palms touching.

You — Point out with your index finger.

Wherever — Point your index finger and shake your hand back and forth. Then hold both hands with the palms facing up. Brush the fingertips of one hand with the fingertips of your other hand. Repeat the motion several times.

You — Point out with your index finger.

Go — Point your index fingers on both hands. Roll one hand forward over the other.

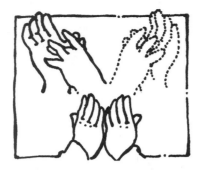

Serve the LORD with all your heart.

1 Samuel 12:20

10/29 – 11/5

Serve — Hold both hands palms up. Alternate moving your hands back and forth in front of your body.

LORD — Make an "L" with the right index finger and thumb. Place the "L" at the left shoulder and then move the "L" across the body to the right waist.

All — Hold the left palm toward the body. Circle the right hand out and around the left palm. End with the back of the right hand in the open left hand.

Heart — Draw an outline of a heart on the chest using the index fingers.

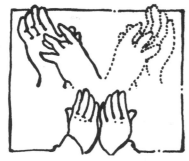

O give thanks to the LORD.

1 Chronicles 16:34

BIBLE VERSE:

Give — Touch your fingers and thumb together on each hand. The palms of the hands should face each other. Move the hands forward and open the fingers so that the palms face up.

Give

Thanks — Touch the fingertips to the lips and then move the hands down and back, one at a time.

Thanks

LORD — Make an "L" with the right index finger and thumb. Place the "L" at the left shoulder and then move the "L" across the body to the right waist.

Lord

BIBLE VERSE:

O LORD, our Lord, your greatness is seen in all the world!

Psalm 8:1, *Good News Bible*

LORD — Make an "L" with the right index finger and thumb. Place the "L" at the left shoulder and then move the "L" across the body to the right waist.

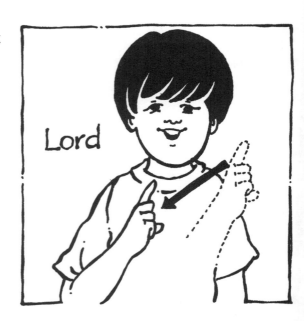

Lord

Greatness — Raise both hands up with palms facing forward.

Seen — Hold your fingers in a V-shape in front of your eyes. Move the hand forward.

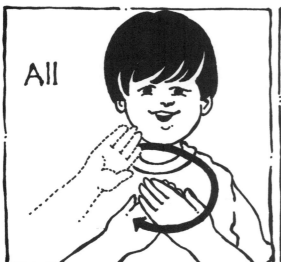

All — Hold the left palm toward the body. Circle the right hand out and around the left palm. End with the back of the right hand in the open left hand.

World — Hold out three fingers on each hand (like a sideways W). Circle the right hand around the left hand. End with the little-finger side of the right hand on the thumb of the left hand.

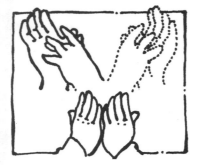

BIBLE VERSE:

I will tell of all the wonderful things God has done.

Psalm 9:1, *Good News Bible*, adapted

I — Hold up the little finger, with the other fingers curled down. Place the hand at the chest.

Tell — Hold your index finger at your chin. Move your finger forward and down.

All — Hold the left palm toward the body. Circle the right hand out and around the left palm. End with the back of the right hand in the open left hand.

Wonderful — Raise both hands up with the palms facing forward.

Things — Hold your hand in front of the body, with the palm up. Move your palm to the right and bounce it slightly.

God — Point the index finger of your right hand, with the other fingers curled down. Bring the hand down and open the palm.

Done — Form a "C" with each hand, with the palms facing down. Move your hands right and left several times.

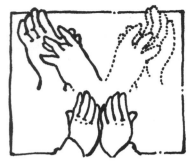

BIBLE VERSE:

The heavens are telling the glory of God.

Psalm 19:1

Heavens — Hold your palm toward your face, just over your head. Sweep your palm from left to right over your head.

Telling — Hold your index finger at your chin. Move your finger forward and down.

Glory — Clap your right hand on the open palm of your left hand. Then move your right hand up in an arc to the front of your right shoulder. Shake your hand as you move it.

God — Point the index finger of your right hand, with the other fingers curled down. Bring the hand down and open the palm.

Heavens

Telling

Glory

God

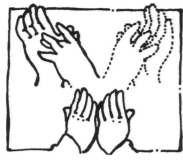

BIBLE VERSE:

O taste and see that the LORD is good.

Psalm 34:8

Taste — Touch the tip of your tongue with the middle finger of your right hand.

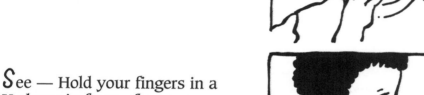

Taste

See — Hold your fingers in a V-shape in front of your eyes. Move the hand forward.

See

LORD — Make an "L" with the right index finger and thumb. Place the "L" at the left shoulder and then move the "L" across the body to the right waist.

Lord

Good — Touch the fingers of your right hand to the lips. Move the hand forward and drop it into the open palm of the left hand.

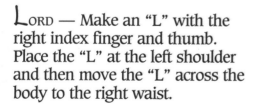

Good

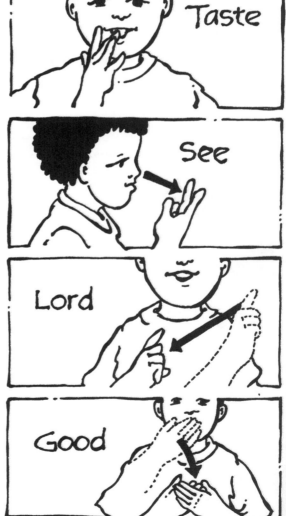

BIBLE VERSE:

Clap your hands, all you peoples; shout to God with loud songs of joy.

Psalm 47:1

Clap — Clap your hands several times.

Hands — Use your right hand to stroke the back of your left hand. Then reverse.

All — Hold the left palm toward the body. Circle the right hand out and around the left palm. End with the back of the right hand in the open left hand.

Peoples — Touch the middle finger to the thumb on each hand. Circle your hands toward the center of your body with alternating motions.

Shout — Make a "C" shape with your right hand and place it in front of your mouth. Move your hand slightly up and to the side.

God — Point the index finger of your right hand, with the other fingers curled down. Bring the hand down and open the palm.

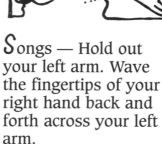

Loud — Touch your ear with your index finger. Then make fists with both hands and shake them back and forth in front of your body.

Songs — Hold out your left arm. Wave the fingertips of your right hand back and forth across your left arm.

Joy — Open both hands, with palms facing the chest. Pat the chest several times while moving the hands upward.

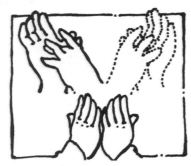

BIBLE VERSE:

God fills my life with good things.

Psalm 103:5,

Good News Bible, adapted

God — Point the index finger of your right hand, with the other fingers curled down. Bring the hand down and open the palm.

God

Fills — Hold your left hand in a fist with the thumb on the outside. Hold your right hand with the palm down. Brush your palm to the left over your fist.

Life — Hold each hand in an "L" shape. Move the "L" hands up the body from the waist to the chest.

Good — Touch the fingers of the right hand to the lips. Move the hand down and place it palm up in the left hand.

Things — Hold your hand in front of your body, with the palm up. Move your palm to the right and bounce it slightly.

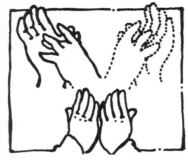

BIBLE VERSE:

This is the day that the LORD has made; let us rejoice and be glad in it.

Psalm 118:24

Day — Extend the index finger of the right hand. Hold the left arm parallel to the floor. Place the right elbow at the left index finger. Move the right index finger in an arc until it touches the inside of the left elbow.

Day

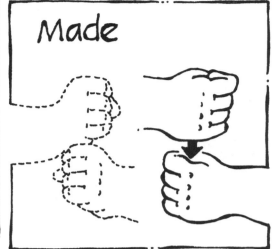

Lord — Make an "L" with the right index finger and thumb. Place the "L" at the left shoulder and then move the "L" across the body to the right waist.

Made — Make fists with both hands, with the thumbs out. Place the right fist on top of the left fist. Turn your fists so that the palms are facing your body. Pound the fists together again. Repeat the motion.

Rejoice and Glad — Open both hands, with the palms facing the chest. Pat the chest several times while moving the hands upward.

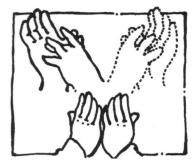

BIBLE VERSE:

Children are a gift from the LORD.

Psalm 127:3, *Good News Bible*

Children — Hold one hand palm down. Pretend to pat the head of a child. Repeat the motion several times.

Gift — Make fists with both hands, with the thumbs outside the fists. Hold the fists so that the palms face each other. Move the hands forward in an arc.

Lord — Make an "L" with the right index finger and thumb. Place the "L" at the left shoulder and then move the "L" across the body to the right waist.

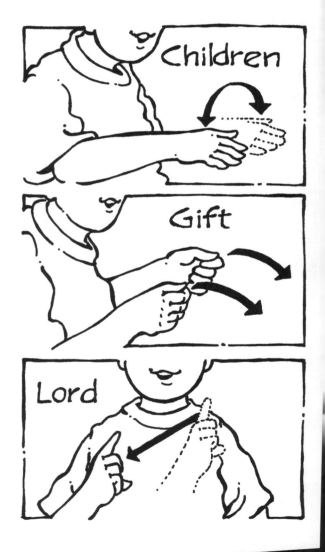

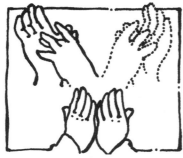

BIBLE VERSE:

Let everything that breathes praise the LORD!

Psalm 150:6

Everything — Make fists with both hands, with the thumbs out. Hold your fists so that the palms face each other. Use the thumb of the right hand to stroke down the thumb of the left hand. Then hold your hand in front of your body, with the palm up. Move your palm to the right and drop it slightly.

Breathes — Hold both hands open in front of the chest with the palms facing the chest. Move the hands in and out.

Praise — Clap your hands several times.

Lord — Make an "L" with the right index finger and thumb. Place the "L" at the left shoulder and then move the "L" across the body to the right waist.

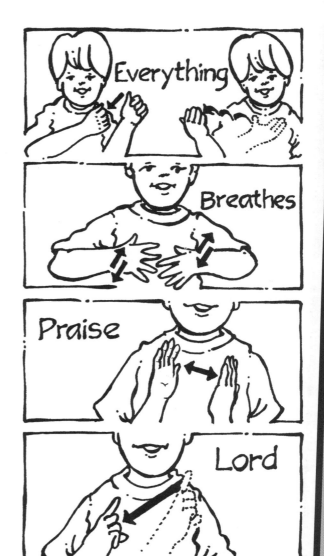

Everything

Breathes

Praise

Lord

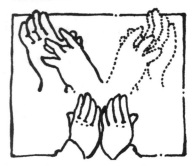

BIBLE VERSE:

Do not fear, for God is with you.

Isaiah 41:10, adapted

Do not — Make a fist with the right hand, with the thumb out. Place the thumb of the fisted hand under the chin. Move the hand forward.

Do not

28

Fear — Hold both hands up with fingers spread, with the palms facing out. The right hand should be slightly behind the left hand. Bring both hands towards the body with a shaking motion.

God — Point the index finger of your right hand, with the other fingers curled down. Bring the hand down and open the palm.

With — Hold both hands in fists, with the thumbs on the outside. Place the fists together, with the palms touching.

You — Point out with your index finger.

BIBLE VERSE:

And remember, I am with you always.
Matthew 28:20

Remember — Curl both hands into fists with the thumbs out. Touch the right thumb to your forehead. Bring your right fist down alongside of your face and then place your right thumb on top of your left thumb.

Remember

I— Hold up the little finger, with the other fingers curled down. Place the hand at the chest.

With — Hold both hands in fists, with the thumbs on the outside. Place the fists together, with the palms touching.

You — Point out with your index finger.

Always — Hold out your index finger with the palm facing up. Draw a circle in front of your body.

31

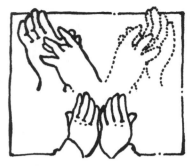

BIBLE VERSE:

Blessed is the one who comes in the name of the Lord!

Mark 11:9

Blessed — Make fists with both hands, with the thumbs out. Place both fists at the mouth. Bring the hands forward and down, opening the hands with the palms down.

Blessed

One — Hold up your index finger.

Comes — Extend the index fingers of both hands. Move the fingers toward the body as they rotate around each other once.

Name — Extend the first two fingers of both hands. Place the fingers of the right hand across the fingers of the left hand, forming an X.

Lord — Make an "L" with the right index finger and thumb. Place the "L" at the left shoulder and then move the "L" across the body to the right waist.

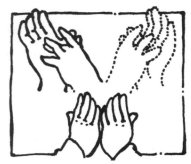

BIBLE VERSE:

I am the light of the world.

John 8:12

I am

the light

of the world.

I — Hold up the little finger, with the other fingers curled down. Place the hand at the chest.

Light — Bring both hands in front of your body, with the finger-tips touching the thumbs. Move the hands up and apart in front of each shoulder. Open the hands and spread the fingers apart as you move.

World — Hold out three fingers on each hand (like a sideways W). Circle the right hand around the left hand. End with the little-finger side of the right hand on the thumb of the left hand.

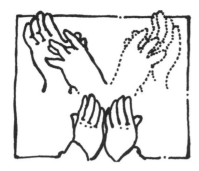

They all shared with one another.

Acts 4:32, *Good News Bible*

BIBLE VERSE:

All — Hold the left palm toward the body. Circle the right hand out and around the left palm. End with the back of the right hand in the open left hand.

Shared — Hold out the left hand, with the palm up. Move the little finger side of the right hand back and forth across the left palm.

One another — Make fists with both hands, with the thumbs out. Hold the right fist with the thumb down. Hold the left fist with the thumb up. Circle the thumbs counter-clockwise around each other.

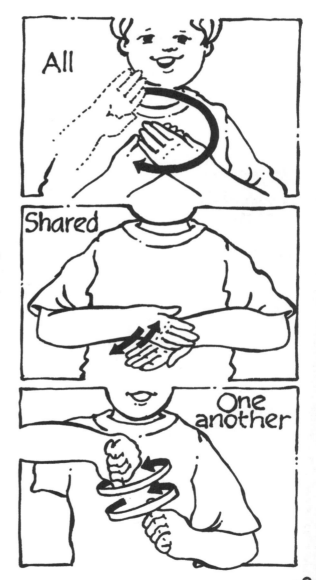

All

Shared

One another

BIBLE VERSE:

Jesus went about doing good.

Acts 10:38, adapted

Jesus — Touch the middle finger of the right hand to the palm of the left hand. Reverse.

Went — Point the index fingers of both hands. Roll one hand forward over the other.

Doing — Form a "C" with each hand, with the palms facing down. Move your hands right and left several times.

Good — Touch the fingers of your right hand to the lips. Move the hand forward and drop it into the open palm of the left hand.

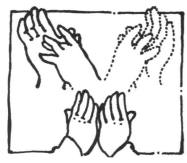

BIBLE VERSE:

Love one another warmly as Christians.

Romans 12:10, *Good News Bible*

Love — Cross your hands at the wrists and press them over your heart.

One another — Make fists with both hands, with the thumbs out. Hold the right fist with the thumb down. Hold the left fist with the thumb up. Circle the thumbs counterclockwise around each other.

Christians — Make a "C" with the right hand. Place the "C" at your left shoulder and move it across your body to the right waist.

Hold both hands in front of your body with the palms facing each other. Bring both hands straight down.

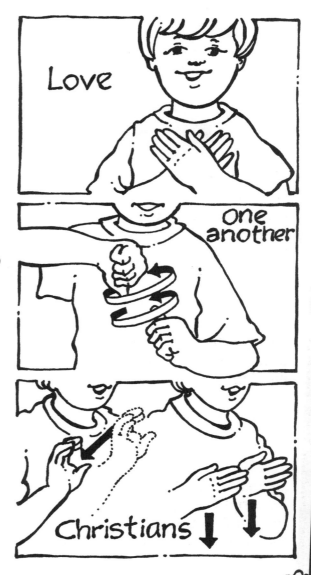

BIBLE VERSE:

Pray at all times.

Romans 12:12, *Good News Bible*

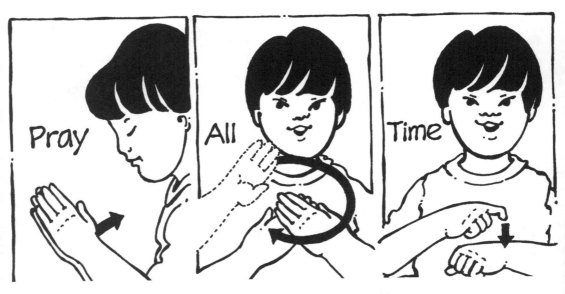

Pray

All

Time

Pray — Place hands palm to palm. Bring your palms toward you and bow your head.

All — Hold the left palm toward the body. Circle the right hand out and around the left palm. End with the back of the right hand in the open left hand.

Times — Use the index finger of your right hand to tap the back of the left hand.

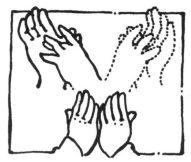

God loves a cheerful giver.

2 Corinthians 9:7

BIBLE VERSE:

God — Point the index finger of your right hand, with the other fingers curled down. Bring the hand down and open the palm.

Loves — Cross your hands at the wrists and press them over your heart.

Cheerful — Hold your hands with the fingers spread apart near the sides of your mouth. Wiggle your fingers as you move your hands up toward your ears.

Giver — Touch your fingers and thumb together on each hand. The palms of the hands should face each other. Move the hands forward and open the fingers so that the palms face up.

Hold both hands in front of your body with the palms facing each other. Bring both hands straight down.

Do good to everyone.

Galatians 6:10, *Good News Bible*

BIBLE VERSE:

Do —Form a "C" with each hand, with the palms facing down. Move your hands right and left several times.

Good — Touch the fingers of your right hand to the lips. Move the hand forward and drop it into the open palm of the left hand.

To — Hold up the index finger of your left hand. Move the index finger of your right hand to touch the index finger of your left hand.

Everyone — Make fists with both hands, with the thumbs out. Hold your fists so that the palms face each other. Use the thumb of the right hand to stroke down the thumb of the left hand.

Then hold up your index finger.

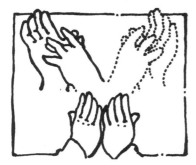

Children, obey your parents.

Ephesians 6:1

BIBLE VERSE:

Children — Hold one hand palm down. Pretend to pat the head of a child. Repeat the action several times.

Children

Obey — Hold both hands in fists at eye level with the palms facing your body. Drop both hands down and open the fists with the palms facing up.

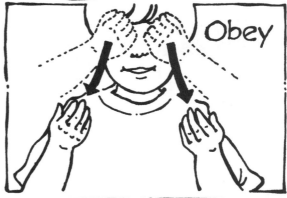

Obey

Parents — Make the signs for *father* and *mother*. **Father:** hold your right hand with the fingers spread apart. Touch the tip of the thumb to your forehead two times. **Mother:** hold your right hand with the fingers spread apart. Touch the tip of the thumb to your chin two times.

Parents

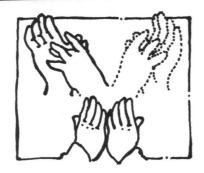

BIBLE VERSE:

I can do all things through Christ who strengthens me.

Philippians 4:13, adapted

I

Do

All

I — Hold up the little finger, with the other fingers curled down. Place the hand at the chest.

Do — Form a "C" with each hand, with the palms facing down. Move your hands right and left several times.

All — Hold the left palm toward the body. Circle the right hand out and around the left palm. End with the back of the right hand in the open left hand.

Things — Hold your hand in front of the body, with the palm up. Move your palm to the right and bounce it slightly.

Christ — Make a "C" with the right hand. Place the "C" at your left shoulder and move it across your body to the right waist.

Strengthens — Touch your fingers to the front of your shoulders. Then bring both hands forward and form fists.

Me — Point the index finger of your right hand toward your chest.

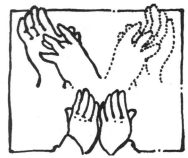

BIBLE VERSE:

For everything created by God is good.

1 Timothy 4:4

Everything — Make fists with both hands, with the thumbs out. Hold your fists so that the palms face each other. Use the thumb of the right hand to stroke down the thumb of the left hand. Then hold your hand in front of the body, with the palm up. Move your palm to the right and drop it slightly.

Created (made) — Make fists with both hands, with the thumbs out. Place the right fist on top of the left fist. Turn your fists so that the palms are facing your body. Pound the fists together again. Repeat the motion.

God — Point the index finger of your right hand, with the other fingers curled down. Bring the hand down and open the palm.

Good — Touch the fingers of your right hand to the lips. Move the hand forward and drop it into the open palm of the left hand.

Everything

Created

God

Good

BIBLE VERSE:

Share what you have.

Hebrews 13:16

Share

You

Have

Share — Hold out the left hand, with the palm up. Move the little finger side of the right hand back and forth across the left palm.

You — Point out with your index finger.

Have — Hold both hands with the fingers bent. Touch the finger-tips to your chest.

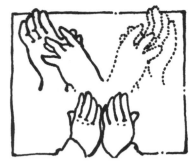

We are God's children.

1 John 3:2

We — Touch your right index finger to your right shoulder. Circle the finger out and then touch it to your left shoulder.

We

God — Point the index finger of your right hand, with the other fingers curled down. Bring the hand down and open the palm.

God

Children — Hold one hand palm down. Pretend to pat the head of a child. Repeat the motion several times.

Children

Alphabetical Index

Scripture Index

Old Testament

Genesis
Then God commanded, "Let there be light."
(Genesis 1:3, *Good News Bible*) — page 7
And God saw that it was good.
(Genesis 1:25) — page 8

Exodus
Respect your father and your mother.
(Exodus 20:12, *Good News Bible*) — page 9

Joshua
God is with you wherever you go.
(Joshua 1:9) — page 10

1 Samuel
Serve the LORD with all your heart.
(1 Samuel 12:20) — page 12

1 Chronicles
O give thanks to the LORD.
(1 Chronicles 16:34) — page 13

Psalms
O LORD, our Lord, your greatness is seen
in all the world! (Psalm 8:1, *Good News
Bible*) — page 14
I will tell of all the wonderful things God
has done. (Psalm 9:1, *Good News Bible*,
adapted) — page 16
The heavens are telling the glory of God.
(Psalm 19:1) — page 18
O taste and see that the LORD is good.
(Psalm 34:8) — page 19
Clap your hands, all you peoples; shout to
God with loud songs of joy. (Psalm
47:1) — page 20
God fills my life with good things. (Psalm
103:5, *Good News Bible*, adapted) — page 22
This is the day that the LORD has made; let
us rejoice and be glad in it. (Psalm
118:24) — page 24
Children are a gift from the LORD. (Psalm
127:3, *Good News Bible*) — page 26
Let everything that breathes praise the
LORD! (Psalm 150:6) — page 27

Isaiah
Do not fear, for God is with you. (Isaiah
41:10, adapted) — page 28

New Testament

Matthew
And remember, I am with you always.
(Matthew 28:20) — page 30

Mark
Blessed is the one who comes in the name
of the Lord! (Mark 11:9) — page 32

John
I am the light of the world. (John 8:12) — page 34

Acts
They all shared with one another. (Acts
4:32, *Good News Bible*) — page 35
Jesus went about doing good. (Acts 10:38,
adapted) — page 36

Romans
Love one another warmly as Christians.
(Romans 12:10, *Good News Bible*) — page 37
Pray at all times. (Romans 12:12, *Good
News Bible*) — page 38

2 Corinthians
God loves a cheerful giver. (2 Corinthians
9:7) — page 39

Galatians
Do good to everyone. (Galatians 6:10, *Good
News Bible*) — page 40

Ephesians
Children, obey your parents. (Ephesians
6:1) — page 41

Philippians
I can do all things through Christ who
strengthens me. (Philippians 4:13,
adapted) — page 42

1 Timothy
For everything created by God is good.
(1 Timothy 4:4) — page 44

Hebrews
Share what you have. (Hebrews 13:16) — page 45

1 John
We are God's children. (1 John 3:2) — page 46